EXPRESS COMMUNITY THROUGH SCHOOLS

EXPRESS COMMUNITY THROUGH SCHOOLS

TAKING SOCIAL ACTION BEYOND THE CLASSROOM

Phil Bowyer

LONDON ● COLORADO SPRINGS ● HYDERABAD

Copyright © 2007 Phil Bowyer

13 12 11 10 09 08 07   7 6 5 4 3 2 1

First published 2007 by Authentic Media
9 Holdom Avenue, Bletchley, Milton Keynes, Bucks, MK1 1QR, UK
1820 Jet Stream Drive, Colorado Springs, CO 80921, USA
OM Authentic Media, Medchal Road, Jeedimetla Village, Secunderabad 500 055, A.P., India
www.authenticmedia.co.uk
Authentic Media is a division of IBS-STL U.K., limited by guarantee, with its Registered Office at
Kingstown Broadway, Carlisle, Cumbria CA3 0HA. Registered in England & Wales No. 1216232.
Registered charity 27016

British Library Cataloguing in Publication Data
A catalogue record for this book is available from the British Library

ISBN-13: 978-1-85078-750-1

Cover Design by fourninezero design.

Print Management by Adare Carwin

Printed and bound in Great Britain by J.H. Haynes & Co., Sparkford

CONTENTS

Acknowledgements   vii

Foreword   ix

Author's preface   xi

How this resource works   xv

Introduction: What is community?   1

Stage one: How to see the needs of community   15

Stage two: How to meet the needs of community   33

Stage three: How the community see their needs met   49

Conclusion   Evaluating the needs of community   63

Support and resources   71

ACKNOWLEDGEMENTS

Particularly thanks should go to Nigel Roberts for his work on the lesson plans and videos.

Thanks also to Dan Etheridge, Alison Farnell, Jim Hartley, Mark Hatcher, Dewi Hughes and Tulo Raistrick

FOREWORD

Express Community through Schools represents an excellent opportunity for schools to engage with their local communities in a way that will challenge, inspire and excite students. By using tried and tested techniques *Express Community through Schools* will encourage, enable and equip schools, and those that work in schools, to find new ways to become more involved within their community.

This material is based on Phil's first book *Express Community*, a guide for small groups on how to bring social action to life, and Tulo Raistrick's *Church, Community and Change* manual – both were produced by Tearfund. Tearfund is a Christian relief and development agency with a vision to transform the lives of millions of the world's poorest people, in a positive and sustainable way, giving them practical help alongside hope, through emotional and spiritual support. *Express Community through Schools* therefore draws on the expertise of Tearfund, the principles of *Express Community*, and the experiences of Christians who have used *Church, Community and Change* to develop a more integrated view of life that sees living within community as their mission and calling.

Express Community through Schools is designed with the government's current strategy for schools in mind. It fits particularly well with citizenship at key stages 3, 4 and 5, offering students the chance not only to explore what makes their local communities work but also a chance to engage in direct action with those communities through a range of projects. *Express Community through Schools* would also make a valuable addition to any study support programme. It would allow for a two way engagement between school and local people. Taking part in such a programme could contribute to such important targets as:

- increasing intergenerational understanding and respect
- building self-esteem and confidence
- building trust
- improving interpersonal and communication skills
- making positive contributions to society.

Express Community through Schools also has a role within the development of an extended school, offering templates for the kind of community surveys and partnerships that lie at the heart of the extended school ethos. It lays an effective foundation for future programmes allowing wider community access.

Whilst the course is written to run during one half term, *Express Community through Schools* contains within it the potential to become an ongoing process within the life and work of the local school. It will help students to think about what they already know about their community, give them tools to connect with their community and, most importantly, enable them to get more involved with their community. It is designed to take the community and its school on a journey that ought to result in some form of appropriate community action, activity or lifestyle change. As a result of completing the process, schools may decide to start a specific initiative to meet a need highlighted by implementing the procedure suggested by the guide; they may choose to join and support existing initiatives of which they have become aware; or alternatively they may feel that for now they have been challenged to make some simple changes to their life that enable them more effectively to 'express community'.

Nigel Roberts, *Schools Resource Manager, Youth for Christ*

AUTHOR'S PREFACE

Working for a relief and development agency, as I do, I'm aware of just how many people in the UK have their basic needs met, e.g. safe water, good sanitation, healthcare and education, in a way that so many people living in the poorer countries I've visited around the world don't. Even so, just because someone is born in the UK, it does not always guarantee they will have a better life than someone who is born overseas. UK youth, in particular, facing difficult situations at home and school, are increasingly suffering from depression, self harm or substance misuse, and subjected to violent behaviour. Even though I am a Christian, it's not just my faith that makes me think that there must be something I can do about these types of problems. The problem I've had is that I've not always been sure about the what, who or how?

Not surprisingly, the best example I can find of someone who was prepared to go to any lengths to address the problems of the people he met was Jesus. The Bible tells us in Matthew 4:12-13, 23-25 how Jesus goes to where people are in order to do his work. Once there, he not only teaches and preaches but he also heals people with all kinds of physical and spiritual needs. Jesus' life was unique in so many ways, but it's the way that his works and wonders match up to his words that particularly challenge me. Often at great cost to himself, Jesus always lived out what he taught: there are not many people you can say that about. So what does this have to do with making a difference to our communities today? The approach Jesus used to see and meet the needs where he lived provides as good a model as any on how to see and meet needs where we live.

1. RECOGNITION – JESUS SAW PEOPLE'S NEEDS

Mark 10:46 –52 represents just one of many examples of how Jesus took time to see people's needs. Although Bartimaeus, the main character in this story, is blind, Jesus doesn't assume he wants to see, but instead takes time to find out what he wants (Mk 10:51). In fact out of the thirty healings attributed to Jesus in the New Testament, there are just six where the individual or a person in relationship with them doesn't initiate that healing. Three occur on the Sabbath, when religious regulations meant people wouldn't dare approach a holy man for healing (Mk. 1:21-28; Mk. 3:1-6; Lk. 13:10-17). The other three are also unique

- Jesus heals a man possessed by a evil spirit, someone in no state of mind to ask for help (Mt. 8:28-34)

- Jesus heals a soldier who has been attacked as he is arrested in the Garden of Gethsemane. He does so in order to demonstrate swiftly that he had no intention of leading a rebellion

- Finally he raises a widow's dead son (Lk. 7:14-15) – this was so extraordinary that it went beyond anyone's capacity to ask for it

On every other occasion that Jesus heals, he shows his immense love and compassion by allowing people to initiate or get involved in their healing process. It is therefore essential if the students you work with are serious about becoming more involved in their community that they work *with* others and not simply *for* them, both in identifying but also meeting their needs.

2. RESTORATION – JESUS MET PEOPLE'S NEEDS

Throughout his life, Jesus not only sees but meets people's needs, regardless of whether these needs are spiritual, physical, social or mental. In the case of Bartimaeus, Jesus sees a need, listens to the concerns of the person involved and then does something about it – he cures Bartimaeus of his blindness. Elsewhere Jesus performs a miraculous sign that results in the feeding of five thousand hungry followers (Mark 6:30ff), he engages and supports those that society is about to condemn (Jn. 8:1ff), he sets people free from psychological hurt or demonic possession (Mk. 5), he heals the sick (Mk. 1:29) and as we have seen, he even raises people from the dead (Mk. 5:37ff). It's clear that on top of meeting the need Jesus sees for people to have a relationship with his Father in heaven, he is just as interested in the day to day pain, problems, concerns and issues of humanity. It's often the small things that matter most: building relationships, listening, offering assistance and serving – they are all part and parcel of the example Jesus sets us. To get involved in any community, it is essential therefore to meet real needs and, in doing so, to make a commitment to make a difference to people's lives here on earth and not just in heaven.

3. RESPONSE – PEOPLE SAW THEIR NEED FOR JESUS (OR NOT)

The record we have of Jesus' life doesn't just say what happens when he sees and meets people's needs; it also tells us how people respond to him. Of course not everyone responds in the same way. Some people follow Jesus (Lk. 5:1-11), some totally change their ways (Lk. 19:1-10), whilst others seem to stay the same (Lk. 18:18-30). As your students engage with their community through *Express Community through Schools*, they ought to expect a similar range of responses. As they step out to love and serve their neighbours, they will respond: hopefully positively. Irrespective of how people respond, what's important is that your students make an unconditional commitment to stay involved in their lives. After working on the streets with young people for a number of years, I eventually decided that, although the way they responded to God was not a condition of my involvement in their lives, I would always include opportunities for them to consider that a response to God was a possible solution to the condition of their lives. Some young people responded positively to God, others didn't, either way, it didn't change the way I felt about them or how they viewed me.

So what conclusion can we draw from this brief insight into Jesus' model for meeting needs? There are so many lessons we could learn, but perhaps the most striking is that even though Jesus must have longed to see people's lives change, he constantly manages to value them in the process. Although I recognise that Jesus' method of serving the people he met represents just one of many ways to meet the needs of a community, I happen to think it's a good one. By using Jesus' three stage approach to meeting needs, *Express Community through Schools* provides a great opportunity for you and your school to take social action beyond the classroom and into the community.

HOW THIS RESOURCE WORKS

Each of the five main sections of *Express Community through Schools* includes background notes for the course facilitator, a lesson plan, and extra activities which will enable students to put into practice what they have learnt. The CD-ROM which accompanies this book contains a range of resources for use within each section. Resources include printables, videos and lesson plans. They are referenced using the type of resource they are (printable, video, etc.), with a number and the title of the resource. For example, the first resource in Section A is called Printable 1: Landmarks.

INTRODUCTION: WHAT IS COMMUNITY?

This section will enable students to understand how a community is formally defined and what is unique about the community in which they live. The following resources and printables for this section can be found on the CD-Rom:

Introductory Lesson:	What is community?
Printable 1:	Landmarks
Video 1:	What is community?
Printable 2:	Community top trumps
Video 2:	What communities are you part of?
Printable 3:	My involvement in community

STAGE 1: HOW TO SEE THE NEEDS OF COMMUNITY

This section will enable students to understand the different needs which may exist within a community and the need for these to be explored. The following resources and printables for this section can be found on the CD-Rom:

Lesson 1:	How to see the needs of community
PowerPoint 1:	Maslow's Hierarchy of need
Printable 4:	Maslow's Hierarchy of need
Video 3:	How not to do interviews
Printable 5:	Listening blocks
Printable 6:	What happened today?

STAGE 2: HOW TO MEET THE NEEDS OF COMMUNITY

This section will enable students to recognise the real needs of their community and assess a realistic response to those needs. The following resources and printables for this section can be found on the CD-Rom:

Lesson 2:	How to meet the needs of community
Printable 7:	Information Summary Sheet – Step 1
Printable 8:	Information Summary Sheet – Step 2
Video 4:	Litter problems
Video 5:	Something to do
Video 6:	Absence of fear

STAGE 3: HOW THE COMMUNITY SEE THEIR NEEDS MET

This section will enable students to understand how to plan and manage a project and ensure that it will be effectively delivered in their community. The following resources and printables for this section can be found on the CD-Rom:

Lesson 3:	How the community see their needs met
Video 7:	What are your communities biggest needs
Printable 9:	Design tasks
Printable 10:	Project roles
Printable 11:	Project descriptions

CONCLUSION: EVALUATING THE NEEDS OF COMMUNITY

This section will show students how and why they should evaluate the success of their project. This should include presentations by students on what has been achieved, visits from members of the community who have benefited from the project, and reflection on what still needs to be done. The following printable for this section can be found on the CD-Rom:

Lesson 4:	Evaluating the needs of community

INTRODUCTION
WHAT IS COMMUNITY?

BACKGROUND NOTES

So what is community? 'Friends?' 'Family!' 'Places you go.' 'People you meet.' '...an assembly of people, a group, a village, or something like that.' We asked people in Birmingham city centre what they thought community was and these were just some of the things they came up with (see *Video 1: What Is Community* on the CD-Rom). 'I think community is...the place that I go to, my college, and my work.' 'A community is ...a group of people and the kind of way that those people interact together.' 'A group of people in certain areas...who are together, who decide things, who come together and solve problems.'

But how would you describe your community, and how well do you think you know it? If you've lived there all your life you probably think you know it quite well. Even if you're relatively new to an area you may still feel you know it pretty well. However, the places where we work, live and play are often the places we take most for granted and think about least. As you go through this resource your role is to enable students to find out more about their local community and its needs, and to participate in projects to meet some of those needs. They may have seen some of the needs previously, but the activities in this book will encourage them to look, listen, and reflect, before they make any decision about how and where to get involved in their community. This section is designed to help students to find out what they really know about their local community.

The only way your students will ever find out more about their community is by meeting the people who form the community they are attempting to serve. Going to where people are will undoubtedly give students more of an insight into what's going on; it will help them to sieve through some of their preconceptions about an area, or even some of the research they may have already gathered. As students start researching what they can do, and why they should be doing it, they ought to begin to see small areas where they can have an impact. Taking time to look, listen and reflect as they begin to go out and touch the lives of real people with real needs will help students to clarify what needs to happen in the community. Most of all, as students begin to draw alongside people it will begin to change them too.

LOOK

Taking time to look around rather than rushing into a project will help students to gain a greater understanding of the area, the issues and the people they hope to serve. Even if students feel the needs are so great that they need meeting now you still need to help them to see the importance of assessing the situation first. Even if your intentions are well meaning, assuming anything about a community without actually checking the real problems could prove disastrous. The people who live in the communities you're looking to serve know the problems and issues that they face; they have to live with them daily.

Picture the scene: A doctor is sitting behind a desk writing notes as a patient comes into the room with a bad limp and clearly in pain. The doctor does look up briefly, sees the problem and immediately applies a bandage to the leg, whilst offering a few comforting words like, 'I'm sure you must have been in a lot of pain ... I know what it's like; having sore shins is terrible. This will do the trick. Let me know if you need any further help,' and so on. The patient looks surprised and a little upset, but every time she attempts to say something, the doctor interrupts with a phrase like, 'You'll be fine now.' In the end the patient gives up trying to talk to the doctor. The doctor finishes the bandaging and goes back to his desk looking very satisfied, mumbling 'Close the door behind you as you leave'. As the patient leaves, looking very despondent, she suddenly clutches her heart and doubles up in pain.

LISTEN

As well as gaining an initial perspective of the issues facing a community by looking, it is essential that your students are also prepared to listen. People will have opinions about the best way to tackle the problems they see which students would do well to listen to.

Hearing the opinions of those who live in the community is both the simplest and most effective way of turning your student's good intentions into good results. This resource isn't just about getting results but about building friendships through which peoples needs can be met. It is important that any effort to serve community does just that, rather than make you feel better about yourself, fill a gap in the curriculum, or help students to get better grades. Hopefully some of the students taking part in this process will live in the area they are hoping to serve which means they will not only know people but will probably want to hear their needs and make a real difference.

REFLECT

You might feel that all this sounds a bit inactive so far, especially since *Express Community through Schools* is about getting out there and doing something. Of course you're right, but this resource is also about taking time to stop in order to consider whether what you're feeling are actual needs that should and could be met by your school. Students will discover this will be a recurring theme; even when they come to plan their community based project(s) at the end of the course they'll still need to look, listen and reflect to ensure they're just as effective in the way they serve people as the preface suggested Jesus was. It's better to take your time than to end up denying people respect and worth by merely doing things *for* them rather than *with* them. Mrs Jones, a woman who has lived in poverty for most of her life, wrote in an article in a national newspaper that 'The poor are so often seen as the passive object of history rather than its active subjects ... poor people want to be included and not judged and "rescued" at times of crisis.'

Whether you and your students consider your community to be poor or not, the same principle applies – doing things to people without involving them probably won't help to meet their needs at all! Local people are the key to meeting needs and ensuring whatever happens as a result of your involvement in their lives has a lasting impact.

INTRODUCTORY LESSON

WHAT IS COMMUNITY?

Learning objective: for students to understand how a community is formally defined and what is particularly unique about the community in which they live.

Learning outcomes: students will be able to articulate the meaning of community, be able to identify the fundamental principles of a community and begin to identify unique aspects of their own community.

Lesson outline:

What on earth? (7 mins)

What is community? (10 mins)

Why community? (13 mins)

Who forms community? (10 mins)

Your community (10 mins)

Plenary (5 mins)

You will need: A pack of coloured pens or pencils per student/small group, paper, *Printable 1: Landmarks, Video 1: What Is Community, Video 2: What Communities are you part of, Printable 2: Community top trumps, Printable 3: My involvement in Community,*

You may need: Printable lesson plan: *Introductory Lesson*

WHAT ON EARTH? (7 MINS)

Aim: to understand that communities often gather around a particular location or defining building.

Activity: divide the class into groups of about four or five. Each group will be shown a picture of a landmark, e.g. the Eiffel tower, the Great Wall of China, the Kremlin, the Leaning tower of Pisa, the Statue of Liberty, the Taj Mahal or perhaps local landmarks from your own community but taken from an unusual angle (see *Printable 1: Landmarks*). If they guess the building straight away, then they get three points. If they need more information show a second, more conventional picture of the same location. If they guess this, then award one point. Add a bonus point if they can name the city/country in which the landmark is situated.

WHAT IS COMMUNITY? (10 MINS)

Aim: to explore how different people define their community.

Activity: keeping them in the same small groups, get the students to write down as many definitions of community as they can think of. After about five minutes, stop the exercise. Tell them that they are about to see a series of *vox pop* interviews with people on the street who have been asked the same question (see Video 1: *What Is Community*). As they listen, ask them to cross off any of their definitions from their list if they hear it from one of the people interviewed. After the video has finished ask groups to read out any remaining definitions.

WHY COMMUNITY (13 MINS)

Aim: to understand that there are at least three reasons why a community might form.

1. Purpose – a community could form in order to achieve something together that cannot be done alone. Some examples might be a football team, the army, a church, a committee. Ask students to give some more examples.

2. Place – a community is formed around a place. Some examples might include the street in which you live, a village, a church, the school. See if the class can think of other examples.

3. People – a community is formed when people find themselves having common interests. Some examples could include a painting class at night

school, a football supporters club or a Doctor Who fan club. Get more examples from the class.

Activity: ask the class to work in pairs in order to identify five local communities. For each community ask students to identify the reason for its existence i.e. place, purpose or people. After a few minutes, feed back. Try to assess what students think is the most common reason for the existence of local communities.

● ●

WHO FORMS COMMUNITY (10 MINS)

Aim: to show how communities are made up of people each bringing a unique set of gifts and skills to their situation.

Activity: Print off, cut up and give out a set of cards to each group/pair (see *Printable 2: Community top trumps*). Divide the cards equally between each of the players. Player one should take their first card, choose a category e.g. community compatibility, and then read their score out of ten. If it is a higher score than their partners corresponding card then they win the round and take their opponents card. If it is lower, the partner wins and they then choose the category. Play two or three rounds.

> **HELPFUL HINT**
>
> Emphasise that everyone in the game had a value and was good in some areas. Together they created something unique that could not be reproduced anywhere else. The unique individuals who form our local communities make those communities unique.

● ●

YOUR COMMUNITY (10 MINS)

Aim: to encourage students to identify the communities to which they belong.

Activity: To help students to prepare for the next activity it may help to show them *Video 2: What Communities are you part of*. Ask each student to write their name in the middle of a piece of paper (see the example below and *Printable 3: My involvement in Community* for a template). Once students have entered their name in the centre circle ask each individual to fill in the diagram like so:

a) In Zone A, write down all the different communities to which they belong or might be a part of, e.g. their family, the school, the local football team, etc.

b) In Zone B, write the individuals and/or people groups these communities bring them into contact with

c) In Zone C, write the issues that these relationships involve or that students are generally interested in, e.g. the environment, counselling, etc.

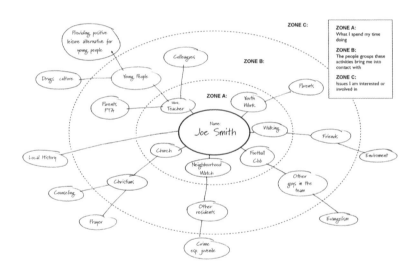

```
┌─────────────────────────────────┐
│ ZONE A:                         │
│ What I spend my time            │
│ doing                           │
│ ZONE B:                         │
│ The people groups these         │
│ activities bring me into        │
│ contact with                    │
│ ZONE C:                         │
│ Issues I am interested or       │
│ involved in                     │
└─────────────────────────────────┘
```

HELPFUL HINT

Whatever students put in Zone C is likely to be connected to Zones A and B. However, if students have an interest which they do not currently spend any time doing but which they still enjoy, they should draw a line connecting it straight to the centre.

Once students have completed the exercise, ask them to share it with a partner. Ask them to think about ways in which they are already involved in the life of their community. Is it with friends at school, college, sports clubs or work? Can they see any communities that they are already involved in that have specific needs that they could look to meet? Encourage them to think about their current community involvement and how they could get more involved by using this resource.

In reality we are members of many communities, where we meet many people and share many different interests. These diagrams will be particularly helpful when you come to think about how, when and where you can see and assess your community's needs in Stages 1 – 2.

● ●

PLENARY (5 MINS)

Ask the class to say what they considered to be the main teaching points of the lesson. Emphasise the three foundations – people, purpose and place. Invite questions relating to the session.

● ●

EXTRAS

Rather than discovering what students can do to their community, this resource is about understanding that everyone is already part of a community. Once students have established what communities they are already involved with, they can start the process of identifying local problems they see in them. As they do so, they should be encouraged to question why these things are issues in the first place. Here are some additional tools to help students to develop their thinking beyond the ways in which they already feel involved in their communities.

DRAW A MAP OF YOUR COMMUNITY

Try the following exercise as a class/school and see what students come up with. You'll need some blank paper (wallpaper lining if you decide to do it as whole class/school) and coloured pens. Use a black pen to draw a map of the community/area/high street, and then use

- a red pen to mark any areas where you don't feel safe
- a blue pen to mark where young people hang out
- a green pen to mark where most people spend their leisure time
- a grey pen to mark where most people work
- a pink pen to mark where the best places to live are
- a brown pen to mark where the worst places to live are
- a yellow pen to mark where you like to spend most of your time
- a purple pen to mark what you would most like to see changed/improved/added

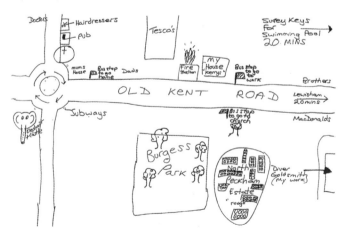

It's worth getting students together with others to discuss what's been drawn. Each of the drawings (or if you've done one big one) will highlight students' initial thoughts about their community and what they think the issues are. It might be helpful to consider some of the following questions

• What did you learn about your community as a result of the exercise?

• What did you learn about others' views of your community?

• How would you use this with the wider community and specifically who with (schools, young people on street corners, etc.)?

CASE STUDY

In a workshop at a church where the cumulative total of people's experience of living in the community was more than nine hundred years, six different groups drew a map of their community, and then wandered around to see what the other groups had drawn. When they were asked what struck them most, they all pointed out the lack of services and amenities in the community (there were no shops, garages, or pubs within walking distance). Even though they had all lived in the community for so long, as car drivers they had never really thought about it before. Then the difficulties that elderly people or those without cars must have in their community, and that their church was one of the few facilities easily accessible. This led them to look on the potential for their building in a whole new light.

TAKE A WALK AROUND YOUR COMMUNITY

One of the best ways to understand what is going on in a community (or the geographical area students are seeking to serve) is to spend time there. Mapping a community will help students to develop their thinking on what they feel they already know about their community. It's probably best to attempt the following exercises as a class or in groups, not only is it safer, but by working together students are likely to get a broader perspective on their local area, the needs it has and how they can best serve their neighbourhood.

IMPORTANT!

It will be necessary for you to carry out some form of Risk Assessment and check out the schools Health and Safety and/or Visit Policy before you plan or embark on any visit to the community.

Plan a number of walks around the community: one route, between one and two miles long, for every four to five people in the class. Make each route as varied as possible, including shops, leafy lanes, housing estates and local parks. Ensure each group has at least one responsible adult with them. Each group will need a map with their route clearly marked. Before students begin their walks, they will need to agree about what issues and areas they would like to think about as they go, for example

LOCAL LIFE

Living: What do students imagine it's like to live in the different places they see: the big houses, the old peoples' home, the housing estate? How old are the cars or even the people?

Occupation: Are there opportunities for people to be employed locally? If so, what are they?

Construction: What are the buildings like: are there factories, warehouses, derelict buildings, new houses or old houses that are boarded up? How old are they? Are they smart or neglected? How do they think this makes people feel?

Amenities: What about the shops? What food do they sell? How expensive are the goods? Do they take credit cards? What are the opening hours? Do they give the appearance of thriving or are they scraping by?

Leisure: What opportunities are there for relaxation and entertainment? What are the pubs like? What about the state of the local parks? Are these places that feel particularly welcoming or threatening?

Litter: Are the streets clean and well lit, or littered with tin cans, chewing gum and cigarette butts? What do students feel about people's sense of pride in the area? What messages of self-worth and value are being given to people by this environment?

Individuals: Look at the people: who are they and what are they doing? What might they be feeling? How is their morale? What level of self-esteem do they seem to possess?

Faith: Note the variety and number of churches, mosques, synagogues and places of worship.

Education: Are there any schools? What kind of schools are they? What condition are they in?

The example is intended as a suggestion. It will help to agree what you're looking for as a whole class or at least allow each small group to come to some agreed method of gathering information. Students may prefer to simply write down the kind of words they would use if they were asked to describe the area(s) to a stranger. The key is to take time to *look, listen* and *reflect*. On their return, ask the students to think and reflect on what they've seen and felt. Ensure they record what they've learnt about their community from this exercise, and what issues the community seems to face.

STAGE ONE
HOW TO SEE THE NEEDS
OF COMMUNITY

BACKGROUND NOTES

Once students have thought about how they feel about their community, they will need to find out what others think. Involving people in research not only means students will be able to get to the heart of their community's problems but it will also give the people they meet the confidence to believe that their contribution is valuable and that they are worth being listened to. Most people will appreciate being encouraged to get involved in something if they believe it's worthwhile. Organising a project and meeting needs within a community means students will have to be creative about the way they go about asking as many people as they can what they think the needs are in an area. It is important that students show a genuine interest in people's lives, rather than simply using their opinions to justify what they've already decided to do. The tools students used to explore their own thoughts about community in the previous section, i.e. the My Involvement in Community exercise and the Mapping your Community exercise, are designed to work equally well with others.

WHO TO ASK?

Working out who to ask and how to ask them is important when it comes to involving people in assessing their own needs. Young people might think the lack of facilities in an area is a major problem, whilst the older people might say the young people are the problem! As students find out more about their community and the issues individuals face, it might be worth targeting specific groups of people they find there, for example

- Different age groups in the community: Children, teenagers, young adults (18-25-year-olds), 25-40-year-olds, 40-55-year-olds, early retirees, elderly people
- Community groups: Sports clubs, political associations, local residents' associations, voluntary organisations, the Women's Institute, youth clubs, parent and toddler groups
- Religious groups: churches, mosques, Hindu temples, synagogues, etc.
- Gatekeepers (people with particular insights!):
    - Crime – community police, local Neighbourhood Watch committee members...
    - Education – pre-school children's workers, teachers, school governors, education welfare officers...

- Employment – Job Centre managers, Social Security officers, local employers, school career advisers, unemployed people...

- Families – Citizens Advice Bureau debt counsellors, Relate marriage counsellors, shopkeepers, social workers...

- Health – Social Services, local GPs, local mental health organisations, local hospitals, people with mental health problems...

- Homelessness – Shelter workers, homeless people, local authority housing officers...

- Recreation – Leisure centre managers, publicans, betting shop managers, social club committee members...

HOW TO ASK

Once your students have decided who they'd like to ask, they'll need to consider how to ask them. Good listening does require a certain amount of skill and confidence. Practising with people students know first might help them to overcome any apprehension. Most students will probably find chatting through issues with friends easy, some will even find it comes naturally with strangers. Whether students find chatting easy or not an informal conversation might not always be appropriate as they tend to avoid the real issues. Interviewing a group of young people about bullying probably won't get students very far – those who are bullied may be too scared to publicly say anything and the bullies aren't likely to admit their involvement either. In the previous section, students drew a map of their community and marked where they felt safe, unsafe and so on. This kind of tool is ideal for finding out how people feel without them having to say so. Here are other ways you could try to get to know what people think:

BUT WHY?

If students are fortunate enough to be able to spend some time with an individual, or have the chance to chat to a group of people then 'But why' flowcharts (see Stage 2, Lesson 2) are a great way to allow people to show how they feel about their area and then draw out the root causes of the problems they've identified. They provide a refreshing change from a traditional question and answer session and the information gathered will be helpful to you in working out what community needs are. People will often be surprised about what they write, probably in the same way that students were when they tried similar practical exercises in the previous section.

HISTORICAL PROFILING

Historical profiling is a helpful way of getting people to think about the present and future by reflecting on the past. Plotting the history of the community or of an issue provides a natural forum to discuss issues of importance in more depth. It is particularly appropriate with the elderly. Although it may generate an initially rose-tinted view of the past, the things people identify as not being as good as they once were are obviously significant to them and worth exploring. It provides a clear indication of their values and what matters to them – an invaluable thing to know in trying to understand the community – even if the factual content is somewhat misleading.

In a group setting it is positive to challenge some of the views, asking the group as a whole whether things really were this good/bad. Ask them to identify definite trends and the reasons for these. For example, tracing the drug culture on an estate over the last fifteen years may reveal a rise in the use of certain drugs and a fall in the use of other drugs. It would be worth exploring the reasons for this.

CHATTING

One of the simplest and least formal ways of finding out what people think is to just ask them!

QUESTIONNAIRES

Questionnaires are useful for gathering large amounts of information quickly. They can also be anonymous (if handed out and asked to be returned) so people can be honest about what they think. Students could drop them through letter-boxes with a brief covering letter explaining what they are trying to do, knock on doors, hand them out at school or youth clubs or simply walk around their area and ask people if they could spare a minute. Questionnaires work with people students don't know and can capture structured information that is easily classified and comparable. Example questions haven't been included in this resource since students can design their own relevant to their area. When students design their questionnaires it is important to remember to allow people to express their views – they already know their own! It is easy to fall into the trap of asking leading questions which allow for only one answer, closed questions that can only be answered with one word, or questions which aren't actually questions but statements of a view with a question mark tacked on the end. Always try to use open questions that help to encourage people to say more.

	Factual	Experiential	Leading
Open	E.g. What is the area like for children?	E.g. How do you feel about living in this area?	E.g. I expect you will have a different view. Would you like to share it with us?
Closed	E.g. How many children live in this street?	E.g. Have you ever felt like giving up?	E.g. Don't you think such a view is irresponsible?

INTERVIEWING

The idea of community gatekeepers has already been touched on in the previous section; these are people in the community who have a real knowledge of the area, key people who hold roles of responsibility or authority. It is important that students talk to a local police officer, head teachers or the manager of a homeless shelter to find out a bit more about the issues they work with everyday. Involving these people in research will be a recurring theme. Students should keep coming back to the people they meet and eventually serve, asking them what they think, giving them opportunities to get involved and helping them to evaluate whatever community projects happens as result.

FOCUS GROUPS

Focus group discussions are a way of digging beneath the surface of the issues by bringing a group of people together to discuss their community. They give people the opportunity to bounce ideas and opinions off each other. Focus groups also give students and others in the group immediate feedback in a way that an individual chat or an interview won't.

There are many different ways to set up a focus group. If students are members of local groups they could ask if they could have some time at the next meeting. Alternatively, students could contact other local community groups, explain what they are doing and ask whether they could talk to the group and listen to their views. Students may have already begun to identify people who have shown a particular interest in what the school is doing during their informal chats, interviews or questionnaires. These people would be good to invite along to a discussion group. Key individuals within the community may be able to set up a focus group, e.g. a social worker may be able to put students in touch with the local support group.

LESSON 1

HOW TO SEE THE NEEDS OF COMMUNITY

Learning objective: for students to understand the different needs that may exist within a community and the importance of exploring these.

Learning outcomes: Students will come to understand that there are different kinds of need within a community and explore ways of assessing need within a community

You will need: *PowerPoint 1: Maslow's Hierarchy of need or Printable 4: Maslow's Hierarchy of need*, pens, paper, *Video 3: How not to do interviews, Printable 5: Listening blocks.*

Lesson outline:

What everyone wants (5 mins)

What everyone needs (10 mins)

What communities need (10 mins)

What communities don't need (3 mins)

Listening blocks (5 mins)

Good listening (7 mins)

Class survey (10 mins)

Plenary (5 mins)

You may need: Printable lesson plan: *Lesson 1*

WHAT EVERYONE WANTS (5 MINS)

Aim: to distinguish between what a person wants and what a person actually needs.

Activity: tell the class that you are going to describe certain objects or feelings. If they feel they really need what is described then they must stand up. If they feel they want it but don't need it, they should sit down (alternatively this can be done on a line across the classroom where students position themselves nearer to one end than the other according to how much they feel they want it).

Read out the following (or choose other examples appropriate to your audience)

- a glass of water
- a glass of lemonade
- a bar of chocolate
- the latest games console
- a boy/girl friend
- a family
- an education
- tickets for the World Cup finals
- love
- respect
- an I-pod
- lots of money
- fame

Discuss the results and see if you can draw out any conclusions. Something we need is something we cannot function properly without. Something we need may well enhance or enrich our lives. Something we want may make life more pleasant, or more fun, but if we didn't have it we would not really suffer.

● ●

WHAT EVERYONE NEEDS (10 MINS)

Aim: to look at what students consider to be the most basic human needs.

Activity: have the whole class brainstorm all the things we need as human beings. Write them on a board. After a few minutes introduce Maslow's Hierarchy of need. This pyramid (see *PowerPoint 1: Maslow's Hierarchy of need* or *Printable 4: Maslow's Hierarchy of need*) represents the different levels of need within communities.

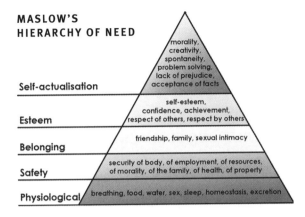

MASLOW'S HIERARCHY OF NEED

Self-actualisation — morality, creativity, spontaneity, problem solving, lack of prejudice, acceptance of facts

Esteem — self-esteem, confidence, achievement, respect of others, respect by others

Belonging — friendship, family, sexual intimacy

Safety — security of body, of employment, of resources, of morality, of the family, of health, of property

Physiological — breathing, food, water, sex, sleep, homeostasis, excretion

---

HELPFUL HINT

Physiological needs represent a person's primary needs, as if these are not met they will cause sickness, pain or discomfort. The need for homeostasis, for example, involves the body's ability to stabilise itself despite external changes, i.e. the way it's able to maintain an internal temperature of around 98.6 degrees Fahrenheit regardless of the temperature outside. It is only once someone's physiological needs are met that their need for **safety** and security begins to emerge.

The third level of human need is **social**, the kind we find in emotionally-based relationships. People can fulfill their need to belong or to be accepted by being part of large groups, e.g. clubs, religious groups, sports teams, gangs, etc. or by sustaining smaller connections with key individuals, e.g. families, mentors, close colleagues or partners with whom they can be intimate. The need to love and be loved (sexually and non-sexually) is also important to this level. When people's social needs are not met they often feel lonely, anxious, and sometimes get depressed.

Maslow's next level of needs involves **esteem**, specifically people's need to be respected, to have self-respect, and to respect others. Any imbalances here can either result in low self-esteem, inferiority complexes, or have the opposite effect such as an inflated sense of self-importance or self confidence. The final level of need **self-actualization** is when someone reaches their fullest potential – apparently only two per cent of people ever reach this level!

Having explained the pyramid, ask the class to place the needs they identified within the various levels. Did any not fit? Maslow has no space for spiritual needs. Did these occur in the class discussion? If not, why not? If so, where should they go? Spiritual needs could go anywhere since in theory they ought to be accessible to people at any level of need.

● ●

WHAT OUR COMMUNITIES NEED (5 MINS)

Aim: to discover methods for seeing local needs.

Activity: brainstorm as a class all the different ways that could be used to discover local needs. Write the answers on a board. Some answers may include – a written survey, an on-line survey, a street interview survey, visits to community groups, open meetings, discussions with experts. What is the best way? If it helps, introduce some of the methods described in the background to this section.

HELPFUL HINT

Nearly all local authority areas in England and Wales have what is known as a **Local Strategic Partnership** (LSP). They are designed to bring together representatives from the local statutory, voluntary, community and private sectors to address local problems, allocate funding, and discuss strategies and initiatives across five key areas: health, housing, education, employment and crime.

Although the LSP is directly responsible for overall strategy and direction, part of this involves developing more localised community plans. In gathering local views and opinions about community plans, your school could have a vital role to play in your LSP. Government guidance actively encourages local community involvement at all levels within the LSP

For further information relating to the LSP in your area, you should contact your local authority. Government guidance and LSP's and Community Strategies can be found at www.neigbourhood.gov.uk.

WHAT COMMUNITIES DON'T NEED (3 MINS)

Aim: to show the wrong way of conducting a survey.

Activity: show the video of a bad street interviewer (*Video 3: How not to do Interviews*). Ask the class what was wrong about the way the interviewer went about his survey.

LISTENING BLOCKS (5 MINS)

Aim: to identify blocks to listening.

One of the problems with the interviewer is that he didn't listen – two way communication is vital in any survey work. Hope, Timmel and Hodzi identify four barriers to communication.[1] Divide the class into small groups and hand out two sets of cards, one with the headings and the other with the definitions of listening blocks (see *Printable 5: Listening blocks*). Groups must match the definition with the barrier. Get feedback and ask the class in what situations they might set up each of the barriers, e.g. in a classroom with a teacher, or in a conversation with someone you are no longer friends with, etc.

GOOD LISTENING (7 MINS)

Aim: to look at simple methods of improving listening skills.

Activity: have everyone sit back to back with a pen and some paper. Ask person one to quickly draw a picture and, as they draw, ask them to tell their partner how to draw the same picture at the same time. Person two must not speak only listen. Compare efforts. If there's time try the exercise a second time only this time person two draws and describes and person one is allowed to ask questions as they go. Compare the efforts. This simple exercise shows that good listening might involve asking further questions to clarify, deepen understanding or to establish greater detail. These three applied with appropriate attention to the person speaking are key skills.

CLASS SURVEY (10 MINS)

Aim: To enable the class to conduct a simple survey of each other.

Activity: Everyone must try and interview as many people as possible in five minutes. They need to discover the answer to three questions:

- what are the biggest needs in the school?
- What are the biggest needs in the town?
- What are the biggest needs in the country?

Students are not allowed to write anything down during the survey but must try and remember their answers through good listening skills. After five minutes ask everyone to go back to their desks then feedback what they felt were the main answers to their survey. Ask if any of those asking questions put up listening blocks. Which ones and why?

● ●

PLENARY (5 MINS)

Ask the class to feedback different examples of human needs.

● ●

HOMEWORK

Give homework – which can be done in pairs – to design a community survey form with questions that would enable the students to gain a good understanding of what the local needs are. Once this has been designed, the class teacher needs to approve the questions and design – making sure that details such as age, gender, area in which they live etc, are included.

HELPFUL HINT

Once their community surveys are approved, students will need to carry out some research within their communities. This can be done either as further homework, using the whole of the next lesson or a number of lessons. A more in-depth approach to needs assessment is outlined in detail as part of Stage two.

[1] T. Raistrick, *Church, Community and Change: The Manual (Phase 2)* (Teddington: Tearfund, 2000), p. 21. These barriers to communication have been adapted from A. Hope, S. Timmel and C. Hodzi, *Training for Transformation* (Zimbabwe: Mambo Press, 1984).

EXTRAS

In order to become more aware of their community, students will need to gather as much local information as they can. In addition to subjective research, i.e. what people feel about their community, objective facts and statistics about a community will be invaluable as students progress through the *Express Community through Schools* process. If some students have expressed fear at the thought of exploring the needs of their community face to face, objective research is a good way to get them more involved in the process. Try to get as many people involved as possible, e.g. other students, their families and friends and even other teachers. Share out the tasks and share findings when you next meet together. Here are some pointers on who to ask and where to look...

INTERNET

A lot of objective research can be done simply by logging on and browsing the internet – which is great if students are into that kind of thing. Simply punch in the name of your community at www.upmystreet.com, or try www.statistics.gov.uk/neighbourhood.

LIBRARY

A visit to the local reference library is as good a place to start as any. It is a good way to begin raising awareness of the local issues. Students will benefit from asking for help in finding out about the particular area or issue they are interested in and a member of staff should be able to point them in the right direction. Sources of information to look for include:

- Ward profiles
- County/borough profiles
- Local authority departmental reports

It is important that students don't feel too overwhelmed by the amount of statistics and information they find. They're not looking to write a PhD but to find out basic things about the area that will surprise and motivate their school and community to take more seriously the issues they both face. What surprises students or makes them think is probably a good indication of what will have an impact on others too. The library should have a census, which contains detailed information about the local community. Examples of things to look out for are:

- the number of elderly people living alone
- the number of single parent families
- the number of substandard accommodation units
- the number of people living on or below the poverty line
- the number of unemployed
- the rate and nature of crime
- the proportion of failing schools; plus any other categories specific to your own community

LOCAL STATUTORY BODIES

Local statutory bodies, such as social services or the health authority, will have masses of information about your community. Ask students to contact the local council, to explain that they are researching the needs of their community, and to ask if they have any studies relevant to their community which they could access.

LOCAL COUNCIL FOR VOLUNTARY SERVICE (CVS)

The local CVS may be aware of other groups who have carried out recent surveys of your community. They may have access to any reports that were produced as a result, or at least know how you can get hold of them. Log on to www.nacvs.org.uk to find your local CVS.

NEIGHBOURHOOD RENEWAL

The Neighbourhood Renewal Unit has a record of the level of deprivation for every ward and local authority area in England. These are available online from the www.neighbourhood.gov.uk

POLICE

Encourage students to contact local or regional police to ask them what community problems they are aware of and whether they have crime statistics or crime prevention initiatives.

OTHER GROUPS

What other community initiatives are already in existence? What is their purpose? What issues and needs do they come across? Who runs them? Are there other faith-based groups doing things in your area? Are there groups that could benefit from additional support? Are there significant needs that no group seems to be meeting at present?

Make sure students keep a record of whoever they contact; they may want to get in touch with them later in the *Express Community through Schools* process, particularly once they have decided which area of action to focus on. Although this research will give students an insight into some of the issues in their local area, statistics can only give a limited and sometimes misleading, view of complex personal situations. The surveys and the tools found throughout this resource will provide a more personal insight into areas and issues of need within your community.

WHAT ABOUT YOU?

As well as statistics and facts, it is important that students record and begin to communicate their own thoughts about this process. A personal journal will help. 'What happened today' is one way students could be encouraged to keep a record of some of their thoughts during the day or week (see below and *Printable 6: What happened today?* for a template). It will act as useful reminder of the people who have inspired them and the things that affected them, the things said during lessons, or any significant observations made about the community thus far. 'So I think that . . .' ought to encourage students to take another step with their thinking.

What happened today

The detail (what, when, where, why and who):

Which left me feeling ...

So I think that ...

Most people find that writing any kind of diary requires self-discipline. Here are a few handy hints to help students get going

- Push yourself at the start to see if you can get into doing it
- Encourage one another
- Do not do it because you think you have to
- Do not try too hard if you are feeling tired

Encouraging individuals to share anything they feel is appropriate from their journal with others at the beginning of each lesson might encourage the whole class to keep a journal. Hearing about one another's progress ought to give encouragement to everyone.

STAGE TWO
HOW TO MEET
THE NEEDS
OF COMMUNITY

BACKGROUND NOTES

Stage two of the *Express Community through Schools* process involves planning a series of steps which will take your students closer to discovering the needs of your community. Although a good questionnaire or well-facilitated focus group will increase the chances of gathering useful subjective research, even these will only be effective if they are part of a well designed and structured approach to assessing needs. A failure to plan your needs assessment could lead to problems later. Start too broad and a lack of focus will lead to a 'wish-list' of one hundred and one needs students would like to address but with which they can do very little. Similarly, if students only check conclusions with a few people in the community they may end up making inappropriate decisions. The approach this resource suggests ought to help students to keep the information gained from their initial research both useful and manageable. You may find you don't need the steps outlined below, you may be able to combine them, but together they represent the sort of steps students will need to take in order to ensure a successful needs assessment.

THE NEEDS ASSESSMENT PROCESS AT A GLANCE

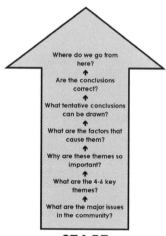

Where do we go from here?

↑

Are the conclusions correct?

↑

What tentative conclusions can be drawn?

↑

What are the factors that cause them?

↑

Why are these themes so important?

↑

What are the 4-6 key themes?

↑

What are the major issues in the community?

START

STEP 1: RESEARCH

You might need: *Printable 7: Information Summary Sheet – Step 1*

The first step of any needs assessment ought to involve asking and listening to as many people as possible in order to gain insight into the major needs and issues which exist within the community. Remember to think carefully about who needs to be listened to. The list of people worth listening to at the beginning of Stage one (Background notes) ought to help here but it is not designed to be comprehensive. You need to match the people you feel are worth listening to with students who are willing to talk and listen to them. Capitalise on any existing links students might have with groups and individuals in the community, refer to the My Community Involvement exercise from the first Lesson. Once students have gained some confidence and understanding of the issues by meeting people they know, it's important they begin to talk to people they don't. If students walked around their community as part of the introduction, you could allocate people according to the routes they took. Once you've decided who needs to talk and listen to whom, you will need to decide how, i.e. what methods will students use with which people? Here's a recap of the different methods available, and when they are most suitably used:

METHOD	BEST USED WITH	FOUND ON p.
1. *But why? flow charts* (asking 'But why?' to dig beneath the surface)	Individuals; groups	17
2. *Chatting* (when an informal approach is best)	Individuals; informal groups	18
3. *Community mapping* (drawing a map of the local area)	Individuals; groups	10
4. *Focus group discussions* (for getting a group to discuss issues)	Groups	20
5. *Historical profiling* (drawing a time line)	Individuals; groups	18
6. *Interviewing* (for asking questions in a more formal setting)	Key individuals in the community	20
7. *Questionnaires* (forms useful to gather a large amount of information quickly)	Individuals you don't know	19

All this planning may sound a little over the top for one project but a quality needs assessment will not happen by accident. Planning:

- provides *roles*, which ensures everyone is involved; you should be able to find methods that match the different skills and level of confidence of each student.

- produces *records*, which should demonstrate a clear picture of what research is happening, who is doing it and with whom. Clear records will make your job of supporting, encouraging and occasionally chasing up students much easier.

- provides a *reminder* to let students know when, where and what they need to do. It should also help to prevent unnecessary overlap, i.e. Mrs Smith being asked about her problem with 'X' by four different people on six different occasions

- produces *results*, not simply at the end, but at every stage of the process. Your planning should lead to a continual process of discovery. As issues or places are researched it is important to keep people updated on the results by clearly communicating your progress.

Good planning is the ideal way to build a step-by-step sense of achievement. You could use the following pro forma to record all the relevant information

---

People, group, issue or place

Who? (person/s responsible for contacting them)

When? (deadline when this should happen)

Why? (specific information you might like to find out)

How? (appropriate research method/s for this individual/group)

Completed (when it was achieved)

STEP 2: REVIEW

You might need: *Printable 8: Information Summary Sheet – Step 2*

Before they can start to identify how specific issues or needs might be met, students will need to review their findings. Collate and sort all the feedback you have so far, either as a class or by forming a small group whose responsibility it will be to do it before the next lesson.

- Count how many people are represented
- Note the age, gender and geographical spread – are there areas of the community or age groups that are under represented?
- Identify the common answers – are there any differences in the kind of answers given by people of different generations or different parts of the community?

Compare this information with any formal statistics obtained as a result of any objective research from the end of Stage one (Extras). Are there common issues and general trends emerging? The lesson plan included as part of this section asks students to list all the different issues and needs identified by the research and write each one on the board, a piece of paper or Post-It note. Students will also need to rank them in order of how important each issue was to the people with whom they consulted. Ask what the majority of people felt was the biggest issue. As students consider some of the results of their research it is important to ensure that nothing is missed, the most significant issue is not always the most obvious. Once agreement on the four or five major themes which seem to be emerging has been reached, try to focus your attention on these, although don't be tempted to start talking about solutions. Try to keep students focused on the needs they have identified for a little bit longer. You may feel it necessary to run any initial conclusions past local people or key gatekeepers. Forming smaller groups to look at each issue you have identified may help to decide

- What additional information needs gathering
- Who needs to be consulted
- What questions need to be asked
- What tools would be most appropriate

As before, each issue group will need to decide who will do what and when. Since the groups might work fairly independently of each other, they may also need to choose a coordinator who will be in regular contact with you as the *Express Community through Schools* facilitator, and maybe even the other issue groups that have been set up. This should make it easier to pass on any information which people feel may be useful to another group and should reduce the chance of overlap. One of the key questions groups must not forget to ask is whether members of the community they consult would be willing to be involved in any response to the needs they have identified.

LESSON 2

HOW TO MEET THE NEEDS OF COMMUNITY

Learning objective: For students to recognise the real needs of their community and assess a realistic response to those needs.

Learning outcomes: Students will have understood the main issues facing their community, explored a variety of solutions to the problems raised, learnt how to assess their own capacity for meeting those needs and have begun to create realistic responses to community needs.

Lesson outline:

Key community words (5 mins)

But why? (10 mins)

Finding a solution (25 mins)

Plenary (15 mins)

You will need: to have prepared research reports, marker pens, A1 paper, *Video 4: Litter problems*, *Video 5: Something to do, and Video 6: Absence of fear.*

Prior to this session the surveys described in the background notes need to have been completed and analysed either by the class teacher, the visiting class leader or by groups of students as part of their homework – a short summary should be made available to the class.

You may need: Printable lesson plan: *Lesson 2*

KEY COMMUNITY WORDS (5 MINS)

Aim: to identify the most recurring themes from the initial subjective research.

Activity: Have the class examine the survey summary in pairs. Ask them to pull out key words from the summary associated with the most commonly identified needs e.g. boredom or litter, safety or shelter. Put these words on a board.

BUT WHY? (10 MINS)

Aim: to help students to think about the possible root causes of problems they encounter.

Activity: Encourage the class to take one of the issues they have identified as an area of need in their community, such as homelessness among teenagers, or more specifically to address the needs of a particular homeless teenager they may have met. They need to ask themselves the question, 'Why is the person like this?' After each answer, encourage them to ask again: 'But why?' and to keep asking the question until they have got as far as they think they can go. Gradually a flow chart is built up going back to the root causes, i.e.

The teenager is homeless

But why?

Because she hated her mum's new boyfriend

But why?

Because he kept hitting her and her mum

But why?

Because he drank too much

But why?

Because he lost his job, etc.

Divide the class into small groups and give each group a large sheet of paper, a marker pen and one of the issues identified in the survey. Ask them to put the title at the top of the sheet, e.g. litter, and underneath put answers to the question – 'But why?' The answer might be because people drop it. Then ask the question again 'But why?' People might drop litter because there are no bins. Again ask the question 'But why?' There may be no bins because they've been burnt or there is no money. Carry this exercise on until you come to an end. This exercise should help students to identify some of the root causes of the community's needs and perhaps spark ideas for where a solution may lie. Use your completed flow charts as a basis for further discussion. You could ask such questions as:

• Which of the causes that you have listed do you think are most important?

• Which of the causes you have listed do you think you can change?

• Which of the causes you have listed do you think the community could work together in changing?

Students may find that some issues they explore are more complicated, and would be best represented through a more complex flow chart, for example

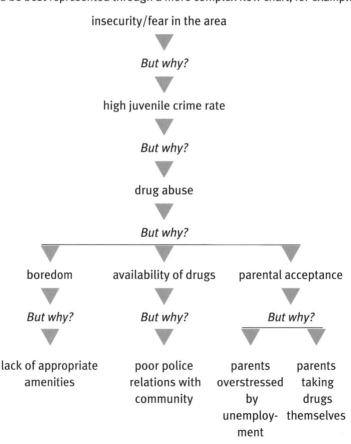

It is inevitable that your students will feel some of the needs they are beginning to identify as a result of this exercise are beyond their capacity to meet. What's important in these cases however is that you encourage students to complete their charts and delay making any decisions about whether or not they can do anything about the causes until the next stage of the process.

● ●

FINDING A SOLUTION (25 MINS)

Aim: to show how extreme some answers to some social problems can be.

Activity: Show *Video 4: Litter problems, Video 5: Something to do, and Video 6: Absence of fear* (see the CD-Rom). Have the groups discuss a realistic solution to the problem they have been looking at. What could they as a group do to make a difference? Ask each group to create a short presentation on a possible solution to their problem.

● ●

PLENARY (15 MINS)

Have each group report back and follow this with a debate on the merits of each opportunity. At the end of the debate vote on which scheme should be taken further.

EXTRAS

By now you should have gathered enough information on the local community and students should be ready to make some initial decisions about what they'd eventually like to do. You've asked students what they think the area's greatest need is and some hard research in the form of local council reports ought to have been analysed or perhaps you commissioned some objective research of your own. Members of the local community have been asked what they think the problems in their community are and what potential solutions to those problems could be. Narrowing down your list to a couple of key issues will help students to focus as they plan their community action initiative in the next section. Before they do, students may find it helpful to develop their vision for their community more formally.

The following process will help students to make a link between the major issues they have identified, the ways these issues manifest themselves in the community (the symptoms) and the root causes of these symptoms. You may find it helpful to refer back to the 'But Why?' diagrams students completed during Lesson 2. Once students have decided on a situation, mission and aims, whatever vision they come up with should then address these three things. This way each student will be able to view all eventual project ideas, from litter picking through to graffiti removal, against what needs they felt needed to be addressed within their community.

ISSUES

To work out a vision, students will first need to work through an issue, looking at its symptoms and causes. It should be obvious what the major issue is from their research. It could be youth boredom, isolation of the elderly or something else. By working back from these issues, students should be able to write down the ways that these problems manifest themselves. For example, if youth boredom is an issue in a community, one might expect to see young people hanging around a lot or there may be a problem with vandalism – these are the kind of symptoms that result. From here, it's possible to begin to work out the causes of these symptoms. Young people hanging around may be the result of low expectations, either of themselves or by others; it could be that they simply have nothing else to do. Vandalism may be due to a lack of respect for other people's property or the community in general – again it could be down to the fact that youths have nothing else to do.

Using the following pro-forma should help your students to structure their own thinking more clearly

Issue	Enter the name of the issue, e.g. youth boredom		
Symptoms	List the symptoms of the issue, e.g. young people hanging around, carrying out vandalism and generally causing trouble.		
Causes	List the causes of the symptoms, e.g. low expectations, limited access to recreational facilities and a lack of respect for other people and their property.		

SITUATION, MISSION AND AIMS

The way students choose to respond to an issue, its symptom and causes will define their situation, mission and aims. By identifying an issue, students should be able to define the situation they have selected to get involved in. In recognising the symptoms of that issue students should be able to work out what their mission might look like. By working out what causes the problem(s) it's possible to make decisions about what students aim to do. The following table shows how by thinking laterally it is possible to turn a negative issue, its symptoms and causes, into a situation, mission and aims which feel more positive.

Issue	Youth boredom		*How this issue presents itself in your community*, e.g. we live in a community where young people are bored	Situation
Symptoms	Young people hanging around, carrying out vandalism and generally causing trouble.		*A list of possible solutions in response to these symptoms*, e.g. Our mission is to provide more for them to do, increase their interaction with the wider community, and address vandalism	Mission
Causes	Low expectations, limited access to recreational facilities and a lack of respect for other people and their property.		*List of your solutions in response to the causes*, e.g. To do this we aim to develop suitable recreation opportunities, facilitate a forum where the views of all ages can be heard, and increase people's pride in their community.	Aims

VISION

Encourage students to use the examples above as guidelines to inform their vision. From their own tables students should be able to write a specific vision that will define the whole, or a part of, their community action initiative. They ought to be able to fill in the blanks of the following sentences:

1. Situation: We live in a community where the issue of _____ is a particular need.

2. Mission: In response to this we believe we are being called to _____

3. Aims: We aim to meet the need by _____

For the example of youth boredom that we've been working on, a possible vision would be:

'We live in a community where addressing the boredom of some of its youth is a particular need. In response to this we believe we are being called to provide more things for young people to do, increase their interaction with the wider community, and address vandalism. We aim to meet the need by developing suitable recreation opportunities, facilitating a forum where the views of all ages can be heard, and increasing people's pride in their community.'

By defining a vision students will be better placed to begin to plan projects, schemes and events that will fulfil their aims. Of course you will also need to ensure that their dreams are matched by their ability to meet them, in particular what resources do you have and what you need. There's no point trying to deal with the issue of youth boredom by planning a youth café with no venue to hold it in or no one to staff it. Even smaller projects need careful planning. A small gardening or decorating project will need a supply of spades, trowels, paint and paint brushes. Does your school have the money to pay for these, are they willing to pay for them, or do you also need to think about raising your own finance? There are lots of questions that you'll need to think through to ensure that your resources match what students hope to do. The number of people available, the funds you've raised or been given and the equipment you are able to use must all realistically fit with the project ideas that you are thinking about.

As you finish Stage 2 and move on to Stage 3 you ought to have sifted through your research and made some initial conclusions. Students should have worked on a vision and asked what is possible by checking that resources match their dreams. Now you're ready to finalise your decisions regarding the nature of the project(s). Again, some of these questions might throw up a mass of issues. However, the next section starts to get radical – you'll be looking at some of the intricacies of actually doing a community-based project!

STAGE THREE
HOW THE COMMUNITY SEE THEIR NEEDS MET

BACKGROUND NOTES

As you get ready to plan project(s) it is just as important to involve the community in meeting their needs as it was in identifying them in Stages 1 – 2. Students need to do it with them, not for them! If the community feels what's being planned affects them or they have something to offer, people will get involved. A project which brings the community together to prevent change they don't want is just as viable as one which brings them together to make changes they do want.

FIND THE RIGHT CAUSE

When some of the material from this resource was used in a Welsh mining community, three different groups independently talked about the 'Gas Tank Wars' in the mid-1970s. Apparently the gas board decided to build two large gas tanks in the middle of the community. Everyone was up in arms about this, so every time the gas board van was seen driving into the village, someone would run down to the fire station and ring the bell. By the time the van reached the site several hundred residents would be standing on the site to confront them. After a while the gas board got fed up and sited the tanks outside the village. Everyone in the group spoke about this event with lots of pride and enthusiasm. When the facilitator asked why, the participants replied that it was because the community had come together and achieved something. His next question brought the significance of their past experiences right up to date: 'What issue today would bring the community together in fighting for a common cause?' For members of the group who were cynical about being able to make a difference, the 'Gas Tank Wars' served as a useful reminder that things could indeed change if they worked together.

Of course if your community feel the project your students are proposing is the change they don't want to see, then you're in trouble! Whether it's phone masts or flight paths, any demonstration of negative feelings towards change students have already noticed within their community ought to serve as a warning to how people feel and are therefore likely to respond when something's imposed on their lives. Rather than impose their own answers to the issues they've identified students will need to ensure that whatever plans they already have for their community encourage people to see how they might become part of the solution. In fact, rather than force people into something they don't want, students need to be prepared to step back and facilitate solutions from within the community itself.

ENCOURAGE COMMITMENT

Ownership will greatly affect people's attitude towards any action students have in mind. Without ownership, people very easily lose interest and become disillusioned and may even try to sabotage a project. With ownership, people pull together, share the burden and achieve the aim in a much more positive atmosphere. Students will need to continually ask for people's opinions, value their contributions, and seek to draw them into participation. Even when people seem to be involved, it is important to keep them motivated, to ensure you don't stray from your original intentions or, even worse, fail to complete what you set out to achieve. The key to unlocking the potential for change within your community is to identify an issue that will keep their and your school's attention, one which you will be committed together to seeing through to completion. Better to do one small thing well than attempt something beyond your capacity to complete.

BUILD CAPACITY

By this stage in the process you should have already thought carefully about your own team of willing volunteers but, as you begin to move closer to action, you will have worked out that it is the community that is the real key to your ability to achieve your vision. There is great strength in working together. Get it right and students will feel both supported and surprised at what can be achieved. It's may be an old adage but TEAM really does mean that Together Everyone Achieves More! Don't try to be self-sufficient. Whatever ideas students choose to use to express community, they will still find roles that can't be filled by the resources available to your school.

SEEK COOPERATION

Of course as well as your students needing your community your community might need them. As well as new projects, don't rule out ideas about projects that mean students add something to an existing group rather than start their own brand new initiative. This resource is about engaging with people and their lives in order to create lasting change (for the better) not necessarily about starting something new. Working with other agencies seeking to meet the same needs students have identified is just as suitable a conclusion to reach as a result of using this resource as forming your own team to do a different task. Don't rule anything out!

Working in partnership with other agencies won't be easy: sometimes it will mean compromise or greater complications but most of the time it will provide confidence and increased capacity. It may mean having faith in the most unlikely people; sometimes it will mean being let down by the most unlikely people. Though your vision should not change, your priorities might. Your agenda may have to be put on the back burner for a while whilst you deal with someone else's pet project. Whether or not you are able to take a lead in this new project, the principles of what makes a good project good will remain. The mission, aims, objectives and activities completed as part of Stage 2 (Extras) are there as a means of refocusing students attention; they will act as a reminder of what you set out to do and who for. That's why it is important that you have them!

LESSON 3

HOW THE COMMUNITY SEE THEIR NEEDS MET

Learning objective: For students to understand how to plan and manage their project and ensure that it will be effectively delivered in their community.

Learning outcomes: By the end of the session students will have developed their final project proposal, understood the importance of careful planning, the value of realistic and achievable timescales and the importance of communication with the local community.

Lesson outline:

Managing a project (10 mins)

Defining the proposal (10 mins)

Planning the project (25 mins)

Plenary (15 mins)

You will need: Pens, paper, *Printable 9: Design tasks*, *Printable 10: Project roles.*

You may need: Printable lesson plan: *Lesson 3, Video 7: What are your communities biggest needs.*

INTRODUCTION

At the end of the last lesson students voted on a proposal for a project. This was only an outline of ideas. This session is designed to ensure that more flesh is put onto the bones of that outline. As a reminder of the importance of remaining need rather than task focused you could open the lesson by showing *Video 7: What are your communities biggest needs.*

MANAGING A PROJECT (10 MINS)

Aim: to highlight the importance of the role we each play in a project.

Activity: Divide the class into groups of five. Each group will be given one of two project proposals (see *Printable 9: Design tasks*). Their task is to fulfil the brief. As well as the task sheet each group member will be given a role card. *These must be kept confidential.* The students must fulfil the brief by following their role card instructions.

After ten minutes get feedback. How close to completing the task are the groups? What is preventing them completing the task? If they did finish is it because one person did everything? The value of the exercise is to highlight the importance of the role we each will play in a project. We need to know what jobs need to be done and then allocate responsibility for each task. This will be vital in the class project – and so as the lesson progresses students need to be thinking of two questions

- What needs to be done?

- Who is the best person to do it?

• •

DEFINING THE PROPOSAL (10 MINS)

Aim: to flesh out the proposal from the last lesson into something much more concrete.

Activity: Tell them that the best way of fleshing out the proposal from the last lesson is by answering a series of questions. Do an example with the whole class, e.g.

A group have agreed there is too much litter in the local park and much of it could be recycled. It is not therefore just a question of litter picking but doing something more constructive.

Ask the following key questions in relation to the example getting the class to think about possible answers. These are the top ten project posers

- What needs to happen?
- How can we make it happen?
- How often will action be needed?

- Where will it happen?
- When will it happen?
- Who will make it happen?
- Who needs to know about it?
- How will we communicate with the community about the project?
- Is there a cost? If so, who will pay?
- Can the project be sustained? If so, how? If not, what will be the impact?

Write out or display the project posers on a board as they form the basis of the main section of the lesson.

PLANNING THE PROJECT (25 MINS)

Aim: To plan the project in greater detail.

Activity: This is the time in the lesson when the proposal becomes a little more solid. Divide the class into three working groups. Appoint a chairperson and secretary for each to ensure that work is done. Give out a brief to each group relating to the project (see *Printable 10: Project roles*). After the allotted time have everyone feedback in the plenary session.

PLENARY (15 MINS)

Aim: to agree a timetable for action.

This is a key time. Pull all the aspects of the briefs together and create a timetable of actions which the whole class agrees with. As each group feeds back, the details and timings will need to be confirmed through probing questions. Once a timetable is agreed, including a start and end date for the project, return to the issue of roles.

On the board will be a list of tasks and a timetable by which they need to be done. Allocate roles for each of the tasks. How this is done is up to each individual teacher. It could be that there will be clear groups able to do specified tasks. Discussion may be needed and the class can choose the roles. What is important is that once roles are agreed, each student is made aware of the importance of their role and that it is now their responsibility to ensure that their section of the task is completed to time.

● ●

HOMEWORK

Students need to ensure that all necessary preparation is done in order to be able to start the project on the agreed date.

HELPFUL HINT

When the project starts, encourage students to keep a project log which will include any letters, publicity, photos, video footage etc. This will be important for the final lesson which will occur after the project is completed.

EXTRAS

By now, you're probably wondering where the list of ready-made ideas for projects is. Although whatever you do as a result of using this resource is about what is needed where you are and not what others have done where they are we have included a list of suggestions of what others have done to meet the needs in their community:

- Cafes
- Fun days
- Gardening
- Dog walking
- Cleaning lifts
- Litter picking
- Music concerts
- Graffiti removal
- Hospital visiting
- Painting murals
- Painting railings
- DIY related help
- House clearance
- Building furniture
- Window cleaning
- Free car washing
- Clearing alleyways
- Cleaning stairwells
- Summer play clubs
- Sports competitions
- Clearing up parkland
- Painting fences/gates
- Community barbeques
- Nail Bars/Beauty salons
- Improving a local playground
- Food shopping for the elderly
- Clubs and dinners for the elderly

- Singing at the local residential home
- Bag packing at the local supermarket
- DJ/Dance/Performing Arts workshops
- Making/delivering soup for the homeless
- Helping the elderly with overgrown gardens
- Listening to readers at the local primary school
- Painting and decorating – one room, one house, one street!

Of course rather than replicate someone else's ideas, the real value of looking at projects others have done is that it ought to inform whatever response you intend to make. You may find it helpful to stick each of the following case-studies on the walls of your room (see *Printable 11: Project descriptions* on the CD-Rom for a printable version of each case study). Ask students to wander around, encourage them to read the case-studies and jot down on a piece of paper:

- How they feel on reading the various case-studies: excited? inadequate? hopeful? unmoved?
- What they think they can learn from the case-studies.

Ask students to feed back how they felt. Explore why they felt the way they did. Ask students what they have learnt from the experiences of each of these projects. If the discussion needs further impetus, you may find the following questions helpful

- What do you think are the keys to making each initiative successful?
- What do the various groups have in common?
- In what ways do they relate to the community?
- How do they make use of their existing skills and resources?

The sort of points you may want to draw out of the discussions will stress the importance of

- identifying what the needs are before jumping in and doing something
- working with the community in identifying the needs
- building relationships with those you are trying to help
- not being afraid to try out simple ideas
- being culturally sensitive
- making the most of existing skills and resources
- involving the local community in helping out in the initiative
- tackling the root causes of the problems

Write down on a large sheet of paper the main points. Ask students what other principles they think are important in planning a community initiative. As the author's own involvement in community work is from a Christian perspective the examples in this book are all taken from projects led by churches or Christian organisations. The principles, however, are just as relevant to schools or any other community group(s).

TOY STORY

A group of Christians in London found that it was difficult for single mothers in their community to get out and meet people, and, as a result, were feeling very isolated. They also recognised that many were struggling to afford toys for their children.

They came up with a simple way of beginning to address these two issues. Every two weeks, someone from the scheme drops in to see the mother, and brings a range of toys with them. As with a library, the mother can return toys and borrow others. During the visits, there is usually time to build relationships and, where appropriate offer further support.

ELDERLY CARE

A church in south-west London uses its premises during the week as a drop-in centre. It provides an opportunity for elderly people, who can often feel isolated in a community, to come together, relax and enjoy each other's company.

One of the things that makes the church centre distinctive is the warm relationships. The elderly people appreciate the welcoming atmosphere, the fact that spiritual issues are not ignored (there is a daily time of prayer) and the fact that everything is done to make them feel at home. For example, most of the elderly are from the Afro-Caribbean community and so food and the activities are given a distinctly Caribbean flavour.

WORK STATION

A youth group from the Midlands recognised that one of the biggest problems in the area was education. When they dug deeper, it became obvious that part of the difficulty was the struggle many young people had with homework. Poor housing conditions made studying in a quiet environment almost impossible and parents did not always have the educational background to be able to help their children.

Consequently the group, with support of local Christian teachers, has set up a homework club, to provide extra lessons and support to children and young people on a Saturday morning.

COMMUNITY SUBWAY PAINTING

A group of Christians in south London is tackling a badly graffitied subway in their area by enlisting the support of the local community. Many people had wanted something done for years, but it was the group that took on the role of catalyst, drawing in the local residents' association, nearby schools, the community art college, and the local DIY shop to get involved in repainting the subway. They were even able to get the youth who had been responsible for most of the graffiti in the first place to help redesign the subway's new look – spray-painted murals, shapes and numbers.

A project that had seemed huge became possible, and has helped to draw the community together. The church made many contacts and relationships with the wider community.

CREDIT'S DUE

Churches in Cleethorpes came together to do something about a local problem – homelessness. They discovered many homeless people caught in a trap. No fixed address meant it was difficult to claim housing benefit, and no money meant they couldn't afford the deposit on the rental property that would give them their fixed address.

The churches devised a loan scheme that guaranteed the landlords' deposit, so enabling the family/individual to move in. Once in, they could claim benefit to pay the rent themselves.

Discovering further needs, the churches now provide debt counselling and a re-cycling scheme that provides new homeowners with low-cost furniture. They're also asking landlords to set a level of rent closer to the level of housing benefit.

LUNCHTIME CLUB

A Manchester group is helping to run a lunchtime club for local school children, at the invitation of the head, after children talked about school bullying at the youth club.

For several weeks, the same group of ten children meet for small group activities, such as drama, games, arts and crafts. The aim is to build positive relationships between the bullies and bullied, helping them to reflect upon their behaviour. Through it, many bullied children have grown in confidence and self-esteem and some of the bullies have learnt to work positively with others. The children have so appreciated the group's input that many now also attend other activities run by local Christians.

RE-CYCLING

A group of Christians in Wales recognised that a key need in their community was employment opportunities. Alongside this, many poorer families found new clothing and furniture far too expensive.

They decided to set up a clothes re-cycling scheme, which very quickly grew so much that they were able to employ a local person to supervise the project. The money that the scheme generated was used to start a furniture recycling business, which not only provided low cost furniture, but also training for local people in carpentry and restoration. On the back of this scheme, a third business was set up, repairing and selling bikes. Again it employed local people and proved a valuable service to the community.

As students read what other groups have done, quite a few are likely to get excited about what they could do; others will be left feeling overwhelmed by the apparent enormity of the task ahead of them. It's worth making the point that there is nothing unusual about these projects. Some are relatively small initiatives, run by a team of twenty or fewer people, so there is no need to feel intimidated by them.

CONCLUSION
EVALUATING THE NEEDS OF COMMUNITY

BACKGROUND NOTES

Evaluation is an important part of whatever social action project students choose to do as a result of using this resource. Whether it is through an official report, a presentation or discussion, this final section will help you to assess what your students have achieved, whether and how to continue the project, or maybe even take the school further into community involvement.

EVALUATING WHAT'S HAPPENED

Try to encourage students to reflect on to what degree the project(s) have fulfilled or at least met some of the elements of their original vision, and in particular whether they met the needs that they and local people identified before the project(s) took place. If you've worked on a city-wide initiative with other schools or community groups, it would be good to regroup and take stock of what's happened through the project and feedback stories, highlights, thoughts, ways to improve, to comment on things that went well and anything that went badly. Document stories, comments from residents, your research methods, how and why students undertook certain projects and where they'll go from now on.

EVALUATING WHAT'S PRESENT

Since you've chosen to involve the community throughout *Express Community through Schools*, from the initial research right through to putting on the project, it's essential that you ask them what they think about what has been done, if it's making a difference or even what they would have done differently. Go back to key people students have served and spoken to and who've been involved, and see if their opinion of the community has changed as a result. Encourage everyone who has been involved in the project(s), both students and members of the community, to come to an evaluation session with what they consider to be the:

- **Hits** (the things that worked well)
- **Misses** (the things that didn't work so well)
- **Maybes** (the things they have questions about)

Ask individuals to be frank, highlighting the strengths and weaknesses of the projects you undertook. Students may find that for some in the community it has been enough to know that the school means well now that its undertaken a project, regardless of whether it worked or not. Being open will help students to develop their relationship with the people they are serving, showing them that they're keen to make a real difference. It's essential that students don't give up but develop and adapt what they've done in light of what people are saying. Encourage people to feed back their thoughts and ask:

- what worked and why?
- how do you know it was a success?
- was it good because of the people involved or because it met a need?
- did the local residents think the project was good?

EVALUATING THE FUTURE

Once you've undertaken a project and evaluated it, there is still a lot that can be done if students want to take the initiative further. Whatever the results, there will still always be aspects that will need adjusting if projects are to meet needs in the area more successfully next time. Ask people about areas they feel require improvement. Ask people whether there were any unmet needs and if so why; whether any issues were ignored or underestimated; whether some failures were inevitable or could have been prevented, foreseen or overcome.

It is important that you, as the facilitator of the whole process, make sure you have compiled an administrative portfolio detailing what you did, lists of contacts, suppliers, venues, budgets, quotations, etc. This will help you to develop future events so you're not constantly writing letters or going over the same ground. This will also help the school take on the project if you move on!

EVALUATE AND CELEBRATE!

It's inevitable that some of your hopes for the project will not have been realised, perhaps it's too soon to expect any significant impact or maybe things simply didn't go quite as you planned. Going through the activities in this section should help you to evaluate what's been achieved. Evaluation is also a great excuse to come together and celebrate what has happened.

LESSON 4

EVALUATING THE NEEDS OF COMMUNITY

Learning objective: for students to understand the need for and method of evaluating the success of their project.

Learning outcomes: By the end of the session students will understand the importance of evaluation and recognise the importance of celebration in relation to a project's success.

Lesson outline:

Celebration (15 mins)

Evaluation (10 mins)

Recommendation (15 mins)

Congratulation (10 mins)

Plenary (10 mins)

You will need: A means of showing PowerPoint and/or videos to a larger number of people, pens, paper.

You may need: Printable lesson plan: *Lesson 4*

INTRODUCTION

This lesson will probably be at the end of a term, preferably not too long after the end of the project. It would be good to ensure the attendance of members of the community who had been involved in the project in some way as input from them will be important in confirming the value of what has been done.

● ●

CELEBRATION (15 MINS)

Aim: to share memories of the project.

Activity: This is not the time for evaluation – that comes later. However you choose to run this section, the key thought is one of celebration – a sense of 'we did it'. If people kept logs or made videos or PowerPoints, show them. If you have a local community person present, ask them to say what difference the project has made. There should be input from any other staff members involved. It may be a good time to give out any certificates of participation.

EVALUATION (10 MINS)

Aim: to evaluate what has been achieved so far.

Activity: Divide the class into pairs and ask them to discuss the following questions

- What worked well? Why?
- What did not work well? Why?

After a few minutes get feedback. Is there agreement? Write a list of the perceived problems on the board for the next activity.

RECOMMENDATION (15 MINS)

Aim: to explore what students would do differently.

Activity: Keep the class in pairs and ask them to consider the areas that did not work well. If they were to do the project again – or if it is to continue with community involvement – what things would need to be managed differently? Ask them to come up with alternative suggestions that might work better. These can form part of a final report.

CONGRATULATION (10 MINS)

Aim: to thank people who have been involved in the project.

Activity: There will be a number of people who helped with the project from outside the school. Use this time to devise ways of thanking them. It may mean a letter. It could be an invitation to an assembly for a formal thank you. Identify those involved and allocate groups to come up with a way of thanks for each of them. Feedback and ensure that these thanks are given.

PLENARY (10 MINS)

Aim: to work out where to go from here.

Is the project going to continue? If so, who is doing it? Will they need feedback from the class in the form of a report? If so, who will write the report? Are there other projects that need to be undertaken? Do students want to continue to be involved in their community? The answers to these questions could well determine the future direction of your curriculum.

WHAT NEXT?

If your project has been a successful way to get more involved in the community, or even if it's not, you may find students and staff want to continue what they've begun. It won't always be glamorous, but try to be as inventive as you can about how to motivate the school to get involved in the community consistently, remembering of course to always ask the community what they want. There's a degree of integrity in getting out and about regularly. The last thing you want anyone to think is that you're doing this once a year to appease your conscience, and for the rest of the year you don't care about the local community! You could arrange some follow up events or plan another project as an active follow-up to your first venture into community.

KEEP CHECKING

If students do want to continue the project(s) they have undertaken, they will need to remember to constantly check and reflect on what they're doing. Referring back to their initial vision as they do so will be essential. In order to monitor and assess progress the school will need to get the people who've been involved with the project(s) together regularly, both the students running the project and members of the community that were involved or impacted. Aim to come together after a month and then every few months, to think again about the hits, misses and maybes. There will always be a range of good things, bad things and 'not sures' on any journey, so when things do not happen as planned, see it as part of a learning curve and ask questions.

KEEP ASKING

If, for some students, it feels like they're heading all the way back to Stage 1, it's because they are. If the project has had any effect, the situation in the community ought to have changed. If students have made a difference, even if it's tiny, and if they plan to carry on doing the same projects, they will see why effective evaluation is essential. Going back to people time and again, gathering research and re-establishing connections between the needs, resources and hopes that are present will enable students to generate more or different projects that meet real needs. The tools and ideas from earlier sections will need to be revisited and reused each time a new project or idea begins.

KEEP GROWING

As well as it being important for you to motivate your students to do more of the same, new relationships with new people and organisations will mean you will need to be strategic about how you take what they have started deeper and further into the community. There are some opportunities that you won't have been able to plan for before your initial project. Students might find that a specific project or relationship with a particular resident really develops and relationships are built. Often projects grow as a result of residents recommending the services groups offer to their friends and neighbours. That's exciting and could take you and your school to new places. If people show an interest in getting involved in future initiatives/projects, follow them up quickly. Take time to share your vision for the community and of course remember to carry out all the necessary checks, e.g. CRB.

KEEP GOING

There are plenty of projects around the country just like yours, which started off as fairly small scale but have now become regular concerted efforts at meeting the needs of a community on a regular basis. As you probably found in your research, meeting needs isn't just about material poverty; it's as much about building confidence, friendship, trust and loads of other things too. It would be fantastic if you were able to keep going, making a positive difference to your community for others, for good.

SUPPORT AND RESOURCES

One of the ways to ensure your project keeps going and growing is to know when and where to look for further support and resources. You may find the following list of agencies, organisations and resources useful if your students are to continue to find ways to express community through schools.

AGENCIES SUPPORTING EXPRESS COMMUNITY THROUGH SCHOOLS

Express Community through Schools is a joint project commissioned by The Diocese of Lichfield and supported by Soul Action.

THE DIOCESE OF LICHFIELD

Founded in AD664, the Diocese of Lichfield is the Church of England in Staffordshire, except for a few parishes in the south-east and south-west; the northern half of Shropshire; Wolverhampton; Walsall; and the northern half of Sandwell. It is one of the largest dioceses in the Church of England, serving a population of 1,922,000 in 1,744 square miles.

Visit: www.lichfield.anglican.org
Email: info@lichfield.anglican.org
Phone: (+44) 01543 306030
Write to: St Mary's House, The Close, Lichfield, Staffordshire, WS13 7LD

SOUL ACTION

Soul Action is a partnership between Tearfund and Soul Survivor to raise up a generation of Christians who are wholehearted about whole life discipleship and mission to the whole world. Soul Action is about people working out their faith with integrity, seeing God move in people's lives, towns, nation and the world and being changed and changing the lives of others in the process. Soul Action is about seeking God's kingdom and remembering the last, the least and the lost in prayer, decisions and actions.

- Join: sign up and receive a monthly e-newsletter with updates which will inspire, equip and connect you to others who are radically living out their faith

- Give: giving money will help Soul Action partner projects to bring life, in every sense of the word, to the communities that they serve and work within

- Go: commit to going into your community or find out about opportunities to be part of a team and serve overseas

To sign up to the e-newsletter, access resources and downloads or find out more

Visit: www.soulaction.org
Email: info@soulaction.org
Phone: (+44) 0870 054 3331
Write to: Soul Action, Unit 2 Paramount Industrial Estate, Sandown Road, Watford, Hertfordshire, United Kingdom. WD24 7XF.

SOUL SURVIVOR

Soul Survivor is a youth movement of evangelical, charismatic Christians. For more details

Visit: www.soulsurvivor.com/uk
Email: info@soulsurvivor.com
Phone: (+44) 0870 0543331
Write to: Soul Survivor, Unit 2 Paramount Industrial Estate, Sandown Road, Watford, Hertfordshire, United Kingdom. WD24 7XF.

TEARFUND

Tearfund is a Christian relief and development charity, passionate about seeing God's justice here on earth. Its vision is to transform the lives of millions of the world's poorest people, in a positive and sustainable way. To find out more about Tearfund:

Visit: www.tearfund.org/youth
Email: enquiry@tearfund.org
Phone: (+44) 0845 355 8355
Write to: Tearfund, 100 Church Road, Teddington, Middlesex, TW11 8QE, England.

HOPE

'Hope' aims to support the diverse range of churches across the United Kingdom who are on a constant mission to serve and communicate with the 58 Million residents and many visitors. Hope proposes to facilitate intensified, united, focused prayer and activities, communicate the Gospel through words and actions and create a lasting legacy of both physical and spiritual change in the lives of communities and individuals, by:

- **Supporting Local Churches** across the UK in their commitment to serve and witness to their communities

- **Encouraging Collaboration** between churches and agencies in reaching out to their communities
- **Resourcing and Training** local churches to develop their ability to engage with their communities on a long term basis
- **Impacting Individuals and Communities** with the Gospel through words and actions.

Phone: +44 (0) 1273 571939
Write to: Hope, Unit 4, Fairway Business Park, Westergate Road, Brighton. BN2 4JZ

CHILD PROTECTION

CHURCHES' CHILD PROTECTION ADVISORY SERVICE

CCPAS is the only independent Christian charity providing professional advice, support, training and resources in all areas of safeguarding children and for those affected by abuse.

Visit: www.ccpas.co.uk
Phone: 0845 120 45 50

THE NSPCC

The National Society for the Prevention of Cruelty to Children is the UK's leading charity specialising in child protection and the prevention of cruelty to children. They have been directly involved in protecting children and campaigning on their behalf since 1884.

Visit: www.nspcc.org.uk
Phone: 0808 800 5000

CHARITIES

CHARITY COMMISSION

The Charity Commission is established by law as the regulator and registrar for charities in England and Wales. Their aim is to provide the best possible regulation of charities in England and Wales in order to increase charities' effectiveness and public confidence and trust.

Visit: www.charitycommission.gov.uk
Phone: 0845 3000218

OFFICE OF THE SCOTTISH CHARITY REGULATOR (OSCR)

OSCR is the independent regulator and registrar of Scottish Charities. Its vision is for a flourishing charity sector in which the public has confidence, underpinned by OSCR's effective delivery of its regulatory role.

Visit: www.oscr.org.uk
Phone: 01382 220446

DEPARTMENT FOR SOCIAL DEVELOPMENT (DSD)

The Department for Social Development has strategic responsibility for urban regeneration, community and voluntary sector development, social legislation, housing, social security benefits, pensions and child support in Northern Ireland.

Visit: www.dsdni.gov.uk

FUNDING

DIRECTORY OF SOCIAL CHANGE

The Directory of Social Change aims to be an internationally recognised independent source of information and support to voluntary and community sectors worldwide. They enable the community and voluntary sectors to achieve their aims through being an independent voice, providing training and information. The DSC has a wide range of directories that concentrate on raising money – where to find it, how and when to apply and what was funded.

Visit: www.dsc.org.uk
Phone: 0845 77 77 07

FUNDING WEBSITES

ACCESS FUNDS

Information on sources of funding for the British non-profit sector

Visit: www.access-funds.co.uk

ASSOCIATION OF CHARITABLE FOUNDATIONS (ACF)

Gives details of members of the Association of Charitable Foundations.

Visit: www.acf.org.uk

BIG LOTTERY FUND

Visit: www.biglotteryfund.org.uk/northernireland
Visit: www.biglotteryfund.org.uk/scotland
Visit: www.biglotteryfund.org.uk/wales

BT COMMUNITY CONNECTIONS

A UK-wide awards scheme to enable local community projects. Awards of internet-ready computers are made to individuals or groups who wish to make a positive impact in their community. There is an online application form

Visit: www.btcommunityconnections.com

COMPANY GIVING

A comprehensive database of company support available to voluntary and community organisations.

Visit: www.companygiving.org.uk

DIRECTORY OF SOCIAL CHANGE

Information about smaller grants is now available online, as well as information about printed guides.

Visit: www.dsc.org.uk

GOVERNMENT FUNDING

Access grants for the Voluntary and Community Sector

Visit: www.governmentfunding.org.uk/

GRANTS FOR INDIVIDUALS

Visit: www.grantsforindividuals.org.uk

GRANTS ONLINE

Information on sources of funding for the British non-profit sector

Visit: www.grantsonline.org.uk

LLOYDS TSB FOUNDATION

An application form can be downloaded from the website, which also has application guidelines.

Visit: www.lloydstsbfoundations.org.uk or
www.ltsbfoundationforscotland.org.uk in Scotland

NEW OPPORTUNITIES FUND

Visit: www.nof.org.uk

THE ESMÉE FAIRBAIRN CHARITABLE TRUST

The Esmée Fairbairn Charitable Trust makes grants in five sectors: arts and heritage; education; environment; social and economic research; and social welfare

Visit: www.efct.org.uk

TRUST FUNDING

A trust-funding database published by the Directory of Social Change

Visit: www.trustfunding.org.uk

HEALTH AND SAFETY

HEALTH AND SAFETY EXECUTIVE

All aspects of health and safety covered, including workplace issues.

Visit: www.hse.gov.uk
Phone: 0845 345 0055

HEALTH AND SAFETY EXECUTIVE FOR NORTHERN IRELAND (HSENI)

Visit: www.hseni.gov.uk
Phone: 028 9024 3249

MONITORING AND REPORTING

CHARITIES EVALUATION SERVICE

Visit: www.ces-vol.org.uk

COMMUNITY DEVELOPMENT FOUNDATION (ENGLAND, SCOTLAND AND WALES)

The Community Development Foundation is the leading source of intelligence, guidance and delivery on community development in England and across the UK.

Visit: www.cdf.org.uk
020 7833 1772

SCOTTISH COMMUNITY DEVELOPMENT CENTRE

Visit: www.scdc.org.uk
Phone: 0141 248 1924

PROJECT MANAGEMENT

CHURCHES' COMMUNITY WORK ALLIANCE

Provides advice, support and resources to help church-related community work.

www.ccwa.org.uk

COUNCIL FOR VOLUNTARY SERVICE (CVS)

Pay your local Council for Voluntary Service (CVS) a visit. Many groups setting up new initiatives have found their knowledge of the local area and advice on project management invaluable.

Visit: www.nacvs.org.uk
Phone: 0114 278 6636

NORTHERN IRELAND COUNCIL FOR VOLUNTARY ACTION (NICVA)

NICVA is the Northern Ireland Council for Voluntary Action, the umbrella body for voluntary and community organisations in Northern Ireland.

Visit: www.nicva.org
Phone: 028 9087 7777

SCOTTISH COUNCIL FOR VOLUNTARY ORGANISATIONS

The Scottish Council for Voluntary Organisations (SCVO) is the national body representing the voluntary sector. The SCVO seeks to advance the values and shared interests of the voluntary sector by fostering co-operation, promoting best practice and delivering sustainable services.

Visit: www.scvo.org.uk

Phone: 0800 169 0022

FURTHER RESOURCES

EXPRESS COMMUNITY

by Phil Bowyer,
published by Spring Harvest publishing division/Authentic Media

This is an inspirational and practical guide to give young people the methods and principles needed for social action. In order to be effectively equipped it is essential to spend some time looking at the Bible and working out exactly what needs doing.

Each session includes Bible study, prayer opportunities, responses, games, activities and ends with a practical application and step-by-step instructions to put what you've learnt into practice. It ends the debate that evangelism and social action are two separate things and enables you to develop a more purposeful approach to serving Jesus in your community.

' My young people are eager to get out and do some stuff in the local area. I can see this being a great resource to capturing some of their drive and turning it into vision and focus.'
Mark Massey, Youth Co-ordinator for Rayleigh Baptist Church

' Packed full of insight, inspiration and some of the best session material any group is ever likely to need...a handbook to action that takes the truths of scripture and translates them into a manifesto for service.' Nigel Roberts, YFC

Written for leaders and members of groups aged 12 to 30

ISBN: 1-85078-583-X

Available online or from local Christian bookshops.

A DIFFERENT WORLD

by Phil Bowyer,
published by Authentic Media.

A different world takes a fresh look at the vital issues affecting humanity. Ready-to-use sessions, activities, games, Bible studies, a video and other resources on the CD-ROM help introduce each topic in a lively and imaginative way. Case studies throughout bring the subjects to life. And at the end of each session you are given practical and biblical advice on what you can do as individuals and communities to really make a difference.

'Providing real insight into the issues relating to poverty, this is a resource full of creative ideas and practical suggestions to challenge and motivate your group'
David Westlake, Director of Innovation, Tearfund

Suitable for use with 11-17 year-olds.

ISBN: 1-85078-652-6

Available online or from local Christian bookshops

THE WHOLE WIDE WORLD

by Phil and Rachel Bowyer,
published by Authentic Media.

The Whole Wide World contains 42 interactive devotions on issues that impact the world and its people. Each imaginative session describes simple and effective ways in which children and families can make a real difference. Suitable for use at home or at church, themes covered include water weather; food, clothes and school.

Pre-prepared resources such as games, photos, videos and worksheets on the CD-Rom and in the Poster Pack will provide you with everything you need. Full of real stories of real people, it will show your family or children's group how they can be part of changing God's world.

'This excellent resource is full of practical ideas that both children and parents will love...invaluable.'
Geoff Harley-Mason, CPAS

'In this great book, Phil and Rachel tackle important issues in a way that is engaging for families and children...simple yet insightful teaching packed full with great ideas and illustrations'
Rachel and Tim Hughes, Holy Trinity, Brompton

Suitable for use with 4-11 year olds

ISBN: 1-85078-657-7

Available online or from local Christian bookshops